MULTIPLE SKILLS SERIES: Reading

Third Edition

Richard A. Boning

SRA McGraw-Hill

Columbus, Ohio

A Division of The McGraw·Hill Companies

Cover, Christopher Arnesen/Tony Stone Images

SRA/McGraw-Hill
A Division of The McGraw·Hill Companies

Send all inquiries to:
SRA/McGraw-Hill
250 Old Wilson Bridge Road
Suite 310
Worthington, Ohio 43085

ISBN 0-02-688424-0

1 2 3 4 5 6 7 8 9 SCG 02 01 00 99 98 97

PURPOSE

The *Multiple Skills Series* is a nonconsumable reading program designed to develop a cluster of key reading skills and to integrate these skills with each other and with the other language arts. *Multiple Skills* is also diagnostic, making it possible for you to identify specific types of reading skills that might be causing difficulty for individual students.

FOR WHOM

The twelve levels of the *Multiple Skills Series* are geared to students who comprehend on the pre-first- through ninth-grade reading levels.

- The Picture Level is for children who have not acquired a basic sight vocabulary.
- The Preparatory 1 Level is for children who have developed a limited basic sight vocabulary.
- The Preparatory 2 Level is for children who have a basic sight vocabulary but are not yet reading on the first-grade level.
- Books A through I are appropriate for students who can read on grade levels one through nine respectively. Because of their high interest level, the books may also be used effectively with students functioning at these levels of competence in other grades.

The **Multiple Skills Series Placement Tests** will help you determine the appropriate level for each student.

PLACEMENT TESTS

The Elementary Placement Test (for grades Pre-1 through 3) and the Midway Placement Tests (for grades 4–9) will help you place each student properly. The tests consist of representative units selected from the series. The test books contain two forms, X and Y. One form may be used for placement and the second as a post-test to measure progress. The tests are easy to administer and score. Blackline Masters are provided for worksheets and student performance profiles.

THE BOOKS

This third edition of the *Multiple Skills Series* maintains the quality and focus that have distinguished this program for over 25 years. The series includes four books at each level, Picture Level through Level I. Each book in the Picture Level through Level B contains 25 units. Each book in Level C through Level I contains 50 units. The units within each book increase in difficulty. The books within a level also increase in difficulty—Level A, Book 2 is slightly more difficult than Level A, Book 1, and so on. This gradual increase in difficulty permits students to advance from one book to the next and from one level to the next without frustration.

Each book contains an **About This Book** page, which explains the skills to the students and shows them how to approach reading the selections and questions. In the lowest levels, you should read About This Book to the children.

The questions that follow each unit are designed to develop specific reading skills. In the lowest levels, you should read the questions to the children.

In Level E, the question pattern in each unit is
1. Title (main idea)
2. Stated detail
3. Stated detail
4. Inference or conclusion
5. Vocabulary

The **Language Activity Pages** (LAP) in each level consist of four parts: Exercising Your Skill, Expanding Your Skill, Exploring Language, and Expressing Yourself. These pages lead the students beyond the book through a broadening spiral of writing, speaking, and other individual and group language activities that apply, extend, and integrate the skills being developed. You may use all, some, or none of the activities in any LAP; however, some LAP activities depend on preceding ones. In the lowest levels, you should read the LAPs to the children.

In Levels C-I, each set of Language Activity Pages focuses on a particular skill developed through the book. Emphasis progresses from the most concrete to the most abstract:

First LAP	Details
Second LAP	Vocabulary
Third LAP	Main ideas
Last LAP	Inferences and conclusions

SESSIONS

The *Multiple Skills Series* is basically an individualized reading program that may be used with small groups or an entire class. Short sessions are the most effective. Use a short session every day or every other day, completing a few units in each session. Time allocated to the Language Activity Pages depends on the abilities of the individual students.

SCORING

Students should record their answers on the reproducible worksheets. The worksheets make scoring easier and provide uniform records of the children's work. Using worksheets also avoids consuming the books.

Because it is important for the students to know how they are progressing, you should score the units as soon as they've been completed. Then you can discuss the questions and activities with the students and encourage them to justify their responses. Many of the LAPs are open-ended and do not lend themselves to an objective score; for this reason, there are no answer keys for these pages.

A careful reader thinks about the writer's words and pays attention to what the story or article is mainly about. A careful reader also "reads between the lines" because a writer does not tell the reader everything. A careful reader tries to figure out the meaning of new words too. As you read the stories and articles in this book, you will practice all of these reading skills.

First you will read a story and choose a good title for it. The title will tell something about the **main idea** of the article or story. To choose a good title, you must know what the story or article is mainly about.

The next two questions will ask you about facts that are stated in the story or article. To answer these questions, read carefully. Pay attention to the **details.**

The fourth question will ask you to figure out **something the writer doesn't tell you directly.** For example, you might read that Dr. Fujihara received an emergency call, drove to Elm Street, and rushed into a house. Even though the writer doesn't tell you directly, you can figure out that Dr. Fujihara knows how to drive and that someone in the house is probably sick. You use the information the author provides plus your own knowledge and experience to figure out what is probably true.

The last question will ask you to tell the meaning of a word in the story or article. You can figure out what the word means by studying its **context**—the other words and sentences in the story. Read the following sentences.

> Clara ran out to the garden excitedly. Vegetables were growing in neat rows in the small, raised beds. Each bed was surrounded by flowers. Clara was not interested in the vegetables. She wanted to see the daisies and the bright yellow *marigolds*.

Did you figure out that marigolds are flowers? What clues in the story helped you figure this out?

This book will help you practice your reading skills. As you learn to use all of these skills together, you will become a better reader.

Few people would be foolish enough to walk among lions and other wild animals. Today you can drive safely through wild animal country, if you keep your car windows closed. There are a number of such open-space zoos in the United States. The first was opened in 1967 in Florida. It is called Lion Country Safari.

Lion Country Safari has 650 acres full of wild African animals. There are many lions and about 350 other animals, such as elephants, giraffes, zebras, rhinos, ostriches, and chimps. To keep visitors safe, there are a few rules—no cloth-top convertibles, all windows closed, and no getting out of cars.

For those who like to get closer to the animals, there is a petting section where there are baby animals only. It's safer that way.

1. The best title is—
   (A) Walking with Wild Animals
   (B) Elephants and Lions
   (C) Follow the Rules
   (D) A Drive-in Zoo

2. One thing *not* allowed in Lion Country Safari is—
   (A) hard-top cars   (B) closed windows
   (C) cloth-top convertibles (D) wild animals

3. In Lion Country Safari there are—
   (A) 640 elephants   (B) 35 animals
   (C) 1,967 giraffes   (D) many lions

4. Leaving car windows open in the Lion Country Safari would be—
   (A) fun   (B) safe
   (C) dangerous   (D) wise

5. The word "section" in line twelve means—
   (A) hospital   (B) animal
   (C) area   (D) glove

Ginny was a big orange cat—a cat with money!

In Keston, England, some years ago, Ginny's owner noticed that something was wrong with Ginny. The cat was limping—limping badly. Ginny was picked up and examined. It was discovered that there were two pieces of what looked like glass in one of her paws.

Her owner took the pieces of "glass" out of Ginny's paw and had them tested. They were diamonds—and worth one hundred dollars each.

On her travels, Ginny had "picked up" the diamonds somewhere. No one ever found out where, although many people *searched*. No one knew except Ginny—and she couldn't tell!

---

1. The best title is—
   (A) Finding Broken Glass
   (B) A Cat with Diamonds
   (C) Testing a Cat's Paw
   (D) A Talking Cat

2. Ginny, the cat, lived in—
   (A) America   (B) Norway
   (C) England   (D) Ireland

3. The two diamonds looked like pieces of—
   (A) rock   (B) wood
   (C) shell   (D) glass

4. After discovering the diamonds, Ginny's owner was probably—
   (A) happy   (B) tired
   (C) upset   (D) hungry

5. The word "searched" in line ten means—
   (A) needed   (B) slipped
   (C) looked   (D) forgot

Would you believe that in Tokyo new police officers take a course in how to use chopsticks correctly? It's true. Tara Falk learned this when she went to Japan with her father on a business trip. Her father's friend, Mr. Sato, told them that the Japanese are really worried about the *decline* in the use of chopsticks.

He said that fifty years ago children used chopsticks correctly by the age of three. Today it may take until they are six or seven. Some never learn at all.

Tara saw "trainer chopsticks" in many Japanese stores. They were made of plastic with loops that show where to put your fingers. From the many thousands sold each day, you can see that the Japanese do not want to lose this old and important skill.

1. The best title is—
   - (A) Chopsticks in Japan
   - (B) Plastic Toys
   - (C) Knives and Forks
   - (D) A Trip to Japan

2. Tara went to Japan—
   - (A) alone
   - (B) with her mother
   - (C) with her father
   - (D) on a class trip

3. When Tara went shopping, she saw—
   - (A) many gifts
   - (B) "trainer chopsticks"
   - (C) her best friend
   - (D) beautiful kites

4. The story suggests that more and more Japanese are—
   - (A) in school
   - (B) eating in restaurants
   - (C) using forks
   - (D) cooking at home

5. The word "decline" in line five means—
   - (A) interest
   - (B) increase
   - (C) lessening
   - (D) playfulness

One day a wild bull moose walked out of the woods and came over to a *herd* of cows on a farm in Minnesota. He became friendly with the cows and began staying around them all day as they grazed in the pasture.

The moose even began eating with the cows, helping to finish up the grass in the pasture. Soon he became the leader of the whole herd. The cows wanted to stay out with the moose when it was time to go back to the barn. Each night the farmer had to chase the moose away in order to get the cows to come home.

---

1. The best title is—
   (A) Milking Cows
   (B) Farming in Minnesota
   (C) The Friendly Moose
   (D) A Big Mean Moose

2. The moose came out of the—
   (A) cave   (B) barn
   (C) woods   (D) zoo

3. The moose ate the—
   (A) cows   (B) grass
   (C) farmer   (D) oats

4. The story suggests that different kinds of animals—
   (A) are always enemies   (B) can be friends
   (C) cannot be friends   (D) cannot be found

5. The word "herd" in line two means—
   (A) sign   (B) group
   (C) milk   (D) single

How many times have you squeezed toothpaste from a tube? Too many times to count? You may be interested to know that it was not always packaged in tubes.

Toothpaste was once sold only in jars—and often the family members all dipped their toothbrushes into the same jar. Not very healthful!

In 1892, Dr. Washington Sheffield, a dentist, had the idea of putting toothpaste in tubes. He began to sell tubes of toothpaste, and business was so good that he *produced* tubes for other products also. The next time you squeeze a tube of toothpaste, think of Dr. Sheffield and his wonderful idea.

1. The best title is—
   (A) Jars and Brushes
   (B) An Unhealthy Idea
   (C) The Beginning of Toothpaste Tubes
   (D) A Dentist Makes a Million Dollars

2. The story says that toothpaste was once sold in—
   (A) boxes   (B) pipes
   (C) jars   (D) bowls

3. Dr. Washington Sheffield was—
   (A) an eye doctor   (B) a dentist
   (C) a teacher   (D) a foot doctor

4. One thing the story does *not* tell about the toothpaste tube is—
   (A) when Sheffield got the idea   (B) who invented it
   (C) how much it cost   (D) if it was a success

5. The word "produced" in line nine means—
   (A) cleaned   (B) lost
   (C) made   (D) squeezed

Did you ever hear of a dog that flies or a horse that sings? Of course not! But there is a fish that walks. It is the walking catfish of Florida.

In the late 1960s, a few were brought from India to Florida. The walking catfish has no enemies in Florida, so its numbers have increased enormously.

The walking catfish walks on its fins. It usually travels at night and can walk a quarter of a mile in a few hours. It has *organs* like lungs as well as gills to help it breathe.

The walking catfish eats almost anything—worms, mussels, insects, plants, and other fish. When its watery home does not have enough food, it simply walks to a new one!

---

1. The best title is—
   (A) The Night Walker
   (B) The Walking Catfish
   (C) Changing Homes
   (D) From India to Florida

2. The walking catfish walks on its—
   (A) short legs
   (B) gills
   (C) lungs
   (D) fins

3. In Florida you can see a—
   (A) dog that flies
   (B) horse that sings
   (C) fish that walks
   (D) tree that cries

4. If the walking catfish had enemies, there would be—
   (A) more of them
   (B) less of them
   (C) the same number
   (D) less cats

5. The word "organs" in line eight means—
   (A) pianos
   (B) gills
   (C) body parts
   (D) moving parts

Levi Strauss left Germany as a young man and came to America. He brought a big roll of canvas with him. He thought he would use the canvas to make tents in America.

When he got to America, he found that people were saying that their pants didn't last long. They wore out too fast. So Levi made pants from his canvas instead of making tents.

Everyone said Levi's *trousers* were the best around, and they started calling them Levis. Today, more than a hundred years later, we still use the same name. We also know the pants as dungarees or blue jeans.

---

1. The best title is—
   (A) A Long Trip
   (B) How Levis Began
   (C) Learning to Sew
   (D) Making Tents

2. Levi Strauss came from—
   (A) Canada   (B) Colombia
   (C) Germany   (D) India

3. Another name for Levis is—
   (A) high heels   (B) yellow jeans
   (C) blue jeans   (D) dumpies

4. The pants that Levi Strauss made—
   (A) were long-lasting   (B) tore easily
   (C) did not sell   (D) were too short

5. The word "trousers" in line nine means—
   (A) hats   (B) pants
   (C) shoes   (D) socks

A boy does not become a man at the same age in every culture in the world. Many people in America feel that a boy becomes a man when he is 18 years old. It is different for an Inuit boy.

In Inuit culture, a boy becomes a man when he kills his first polar bear. The polar bear, which may be nine feet long and weigh 1,000 pounds, is a very dangerous animal. To kill one takes a great deal of courage and skill. They boy who can kill a polar bear has developed the skills and courage needed to be a hunter—and a man.

Polar bears give the Inuit people meat to eat, skins for clothing, and oil for heat and light. A boy who can provide all these things has *certainly* become a man.

---

1. The best title is—
   (A) Inuit
   (B) Polar Bears
   (C) Becoming a Man
   (D) American Men

2. Polar bears are—
   (A) large   (B) small
   (C) fast   (D) tiny

3. To kill a polar bear, one needs to be a good—
   (A) farmer   (B) hunter
   (C) boxer   (D) spy

4. We know from the story that Inuit people eat—
   (A) vegetables   (B) ice cream
   (C) potatoes   (D) meat

5. The word "certainly" in line eleven means—
   (A) never   (B) perhaps
   (C) surely   (D) someday

People have always enjoyed painting and art. Even cave dwellers, who lived on earth 30,000 years ago, drew pictures.

In 1940, four schoolchildren in France made an exciting discovery. They were playing on some hills when they found a cave they hadn't seen before. Entering the cave, they found paintings of bulls, horses, and deer on the walls. Experts came to see the paintings and said that they had been painted over 20,000 years ago.

The paintings were in excellent condition because they were *protected* from the weather. Today, thousands of people visit this cave in Lascaux, France, every year.

1. The best title is—
   (A) Art of the Cave Dwellers
   (B) Visitors in France
   (C) Caves
   (D) Four Schoolchildren

2. The schoolchildren found the cave—
   (A) on a mountain   (B) in a valley
   (C) on a hill   (D) by water

3. The paintings found in the cave were of—
   (A) oceans   (B) animals
   (C) trees   (D) faces

4. Paintings left outdoors will be—
   (A) improved   (B) beautiful
   (C) harmed   (D) sold

5. The word "protected" in line nine means—
   (A) lost forever   (B) kept safe
   (C) outside   (D) discovered

Do you know what a ladycow and a ladybird are? They are other names for what most of us call the ladybug. The ladybug is a very well-known insect.

People around the world believe different things about the ladybug. French farmers say the ladybug brings good weather. English farmers think ladybugs mean a good harvest. Girls in Europe believe if they let a ladybug crawl across their hands they will soon be married.

All these thoughts may not be true, but ladybugs do help farmers. They eat *harmful* insects that destroy crops. Many countries buy thousands of ladybugs to help their farmers. The ladybug is truly a friend of people.

---

1. The best title is—
   (A) Interesting Insects
   (B) Strange Bugs
   (C) French Farmers
   (D) The Helpful Ladybug

2. The ladybug is—
   (A) a bird   (B) an insect
   (C) a lizard   (D) a fish

3. Ladybugs help—
   (A) insects   (B) bakers
   (C) farmers   (D) swimmers

4. Seeing many ladybugs would probably make an English farmer—
   (A) happy   (B) afraid
   (C) angry   (D) tired

5. The word "harmful" in line nine means—
   (A) tiny   (B) damaging
   (C) careful   (D) rare

A lot of people have a favorite dog, and for some, that favorite is the dachshund. The dachshund is the dog that looks like a frankfurter. The little town of Gergweis, Germany, is a great place to visit if you like dachshunds. This town has more dachshunds than people!

The reason for this is that almost everyone in the town raises the long little dogs. They sell them to pet shops all over the world. A woman called "Dachshund Katie" began it all many years ago. People saw that she made money from *breeding* dachshunds. Soon many of her neighbors started doing the same.

You can guess what is the loudest sound in Gergweis—barking!

1. The best title is—
   (A) Hot Dogs
   (B) A Town of Dachshunds
   (C) A Quiet Town
   (D) Making Money

2. The story says that dachshunds are sold to—
   (A) zoos
   (B) pet shops
   (C) butchers
   (D) race tracks

3. The dachshund looks like a—
   (A) hamburger
   (B) kitten
   (C) frankfurter
   (D) lion

4. In Gergweis, raising dachshunds is—
   (A) a good business
   (B) never done
   (C) a poor business
   (D) very difficult

5. The word "breeding" in line eight means—
   (A) seeing
   (B) raising
   (C) cooking
   (D) drawing

There is a place called Pumpkin Land. It's not on the map, but hundreds of people visit it every year.

You can find Pumpkin Land at a roadside fruit and vegetable market near Georgetown, Delaware. Each fall, visitors can see a group of life-sized book and cartoon characters. Their bodies are wooden frames that are covered with old clothing. Their heads are large painted pumpkins. Charlie Brown and E.T. are just two of the pumpkin people who live in Pumpkin Land.

A visit to Pumpkin Land at Halloween time is a *popular* class trip. School children enjoy seeing their favorite characters. While they are there, they sometimes get free pumpkins to paint in any way they like.

1. The best title is—
   (A) Charlie Brown and E.T.
   (B) Going on Class Trips
   (C) The Land of the Pumpkin People
   (D) How to Paint Pumpkins

2. The bodies of the pumpkin people are made of—
   (A) straw   (B) old rags
   (C) wood   (D) feathers

3. Pumpkin Land is in—
   (A) Delaware   (B) Florida
   (C) California   (D) New York

4. The story does *not* tell—
   (A) the size of the characters   (B) who some visitors are
   (C) when people visit   (D) how many pumpkin
                                        people there are

5. The word "popular" in line nine means—
   (A) unhealthy   (B) scary
   (C) not useful   (D) liked by many people

In Unit 3, you read about Tara's trip to Japan. Think about what you now know about chopsticks. Then read the following paragraph.

Chopsticks are handy eating tools that have been around for a very long time. The Chinese invented them over 2,500 years ago. Chopsticks are still used widely today, even though many people in Japan and China are using knives and forks because they want to learn more about Western ways of eating.

As interest in using knives and forks grows throughout Asia, more and more Americans are learning to use chopsticks. Americans use chopsticks mainly when they eat in Asian restaurants. Waiters in most Japanese, Chinese, Vietnamese, and Korean restaurants in America or Canada will give you chopsticks if you ask for them.

A. Exercising Your Skill

Copy the idea map below on your paper. Then under each heading, list facts you learned about chopsticks. Add any other facts you may know.

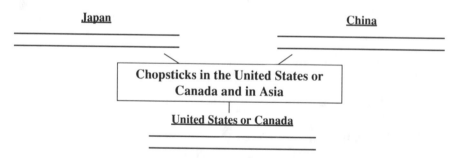

B. Expanding Your Skill

Chopsticks are one kind of eating utensil, or instrument. We use many other tools and utensils. Think of the different tools we use and how we use them. Choose a tool or utensil. Find out more about it. Use an encyclopedia or library book to get your information. On your paper, write the name of the utensil or tool and four facts you learned about it. Ask questions like those below as you search for information.

- When was it invented?
- Who used it in the past?
- Where was it invented?
- Who uses it today?

C. Exploring Language

Read this paragraph about one method of eating.

> People's earliest utensils were their fingers and hands. Today all over the world there are people with very good table manners who follow their country's custom of using their fingers as tools for eating. With pieces of bread in hand, they scoop up food and place it neatly into their mouths.

Think about what you know and what you have learned about the different ways of eating food. Write a brief paragraph. Start with the topic sentence below. Then complete the paragraph by adding six sentences, using facts from your own experience. When you have finished, write a title for your paragraph.

_____ *(Title)*

There are certain foods in this country that we eat with our hands or fingers. _____

_____

_____

_____

D. Expressing Yourself

Choose one of these activities.

1. Draw or cut out pictures of several foods from other countries that are usually eaten without utensils. Write a label under each and arrange your pictures by country to make a booklet or poster. Then add a title.

2. First think about the words you would use to describe a utensil, and then list them on scrap paper. Consider the questions below.

   • What is its shape?   • Is it smooth, bumpy, or sharp?
   • What is its size?   • How did it look years ago?
   • Is it light or heavy?   • How does it look today?
   • What is it usually made of?   • What is it used for?

   Now on your own paper, write a paragraph describing the utensil.

ROBERTS CREEK ELEMENTARY SCHOOL

Egg rolling is an old custom at Easter time. Children paint hard-boiled eggs with colorful *designs* and roll them across the grass in races.

One hundred years ago, children in Washington, D.C., used to roll eggs every Easter on the grounds of the Capitol Building. The custom soon became popular. The crowds grew so large that there wasn't room for everyone who wanted to roll eggs.

The Easter egg rolling was moved to the south lawn of the White House. Every Easter Sunday, a crowd visits the White House for an egg-rolling contest, which is open only to children under eight. Sometimes the President comes out to watch this old custom continue.

---

1. The best title is—
   (A) Eating Eggs
   (B) The President
   (C) Egg Rolling in Washington
   (D) Painting Eggs with Colorful Designs

2. The egg-rolling contest was moved because there—
   (A) were too few people   (B) was too much space
   (C) were too many people   (D) were too many presidents

3. Eggs were first rolled on the lawn of the—
   (A) Capitol Building   (B) Washington Monument
   (C) Empire State Building   (D) Statue of Liberty

4. The story does *not* tell—
   (A) if any important people   (B) whom the contest is open to
       watch
   (C) when the contest is held   (D) if the eggs are eaten later

5. The word "designs" in line two means—
   (A) friends   (B) patterns
   (C) feathers   (D) grass

An insect called the walking stick is often mistaken for a stick. These wingless insects have long, thin bodies and legs. They are shaped just like a stick.

Young walking sticks are green. Older walking sticks are usually brown. If attacked, they give off a bad-smelling liquid that often turns away enemies.

During the day, walking sticks don't move for hours. Only at night do they *creep* along looking for food. The next time you see a twig move, look closely. Maybe it's a walking stick!

1. The best title is—
   (A) Looking for Food
   (B) Many Kinds of Insects
   (C) The Walking Stick
   (D) Walking Tall

2. Young walking sticks are—
   (A) red   (B) green
   (C) fat   (D) yellow

3. Walking sticks have no—
   (A) wings   (B) bodies
   (C) legs   (D) color

4. The story suggests that the enemies of the walking stick—
   (A) have claws   (B) like the liquid
   (C) are small   (D) dislike the liquid

5. The word "creep" in line eight means—
   (A) move slowly   (B) swim
   (C) stand still   (D) fly

A Californian named Epperson was visiting in New Jersey in 1926. One cold evening at his friend's house, he was drinking a glass of lemonade with a spoon in it. He left the lemonade on the window sill overnight, while he slept.

The next morning, the lemonade was frozen solid. Holding the glass by the spoon handle, he put it under running water until the *chunk* of frozen lemonade came loose.

He named this invention the "Epsicle" and started selling it back home in California. Today, this treat is known as the "popsicle."

1. The best title is—
   (A) Visiting California
   (B) A Cold Night
   (C) Making Good Lemonade
   (D) How We Got the Popsicle

2. Epperson was visiting—
   (A) Colorado   (B) New Mexico
   (C) New Jersey   (D) Alabama

3. What we call a "popsicle" was first called—
   (A) an ice cream cone   (B) an Epsicle
   (C) a fudgie   (D) an icicle

4. The window sill where Epperson left the lemonade must have been—
   (A) warm   (B) very hot
   (C) near the floor   (D) very cold

5. The word "chunk" in line seven means—
   (A) flavor   (B) thick piece
   (C) laugh   (D) triangle

The hamburger is one of the most popular foods in the country. Americans eat over 40 billion of them a year.

CBS-TV News started keeping an *account* of the various names for different kinds and sizes of burgers around the country. They found king burgers, queen burgers, mini burgers, maxi burgers, tuna burgers, poppa burgers, momma burgers, and baby burgers. In the South, they ate Dixie burgers, and in Washington, D.C., they ate Capitol burgers. Some restaurant owners named burgers after themselves: Buddy burgers, Juan burgers, and dozens more.

No matter what they're called, Americans eat a lot of them!

---

1. The best title is—
    (A) Eating in Washington, D.C.
    (B) Baby Burgers
    (C) Many Kinds of Burgers
    (D) Traveling in America

2. In the South, CBS-TV found—
    (A) Capitol burgers   (B) pop burgers
    (C) Dixie burgers   (D) Buddy burgers

3. Americans eat about 40 billion hamburgers each—
    (A) year   (B) week
    (C) day   (D) month

4. Since the hamburger is such a popular food, many Americans must like—
    (A) restaurants   (B) meat
    (C) all sandwiches   (D) catsup

5. The word "account" in line three means—
    (A) recipe   (B) hunger
    (C) record   (D) library

What animal has the longest nose in the world? If you thought the elephant, you were right. The elephant's nose, called a trunk, is also the most useful nose in the world.

Just think of all the things the elephant uses its nose for. It uses it to sniff food, roll logs, and fight *foes*. When it is thirsty, the elephant can drink six quarts with one noseful. It also uses its nose for taking a bath.

The elephant's nose is boneless. This makes it soft and easy to bend. If it were not easy to bend, the elephant wouldn't be able to hold the little peanuts it loves to eat!

There are many wonderful things about the elephant, but its nose may be the most wonderful of all.

1. The best title is—
   (A) Elephants and Peanuts
   (B) A Nose that Fights
   (C) A Useful Nose
   (D) Packing a Trunk

2. With one noseful the elephant can—
   (A) sneeze   (B) hear
   (C) drink six quarts   (D) drink ten quarts

3. The elephant's nose has—
   (A) one bone   (B) few uses
   (C) no bones   (D) two trunks

4. The elephant could use its nose to—
   (A) put out fires   (B) climb trees
   (C) sell peanuts   (D) see other animals

5. The word "foes" in line five means—
   (A) food   (B) friends
   (C) insects   (D) enemies

Few people know the meaning of the word "haboob." Those that do, shudder when they think of it or hear of its *approach*.

Haboobs are giant dust storms that frequently occur in the desert areas of North Africa. They also occur on the plains of India.

Moving at a rate of thirty or forty miles an hour, these masses of sand sweep across the land, destroying trees, damaging property, and even taking lives.

Haboobs form when rain first begins to fall. The air, cooled by the rain, then picks up the dust and the deadly haboob is formed.

---

1. The best title is—
   (A) Desert Regions of America
   (B) Haboobs—Desert Dust Storms
   (C) The Speed of Haboobs
   (D) Why People Shudder

2. A haboob is a—
   (A) rainstorm   (B) dust storm
   (C) kind of camel   (D) water hole

3. A haboob is first caused by—
   (A) people   (B) the sun
   (C) rain   (D) giant fans

4. Haboobs must be—
   (A) happy events   (B) very small
   (C) large waves   (D) very frightening

5. The word "approach" in line two means—
   (A) going away   (B) seeing clearly
   (C) coming near   (D) losing forever

Every year, millions of people take trips in airplanes. So do millions of animals.

Animals are flown to pet shops, laboratories, farms, zoos, and *elsewhere*. People ship all kinds of animals, including birds, cats, snakes, and horses.

It isn't easy for flight crews with animals aboard. Mynah birds must be fed every hour. Crocodiles need to be sprayed with water.

One time a pilot found the monkey cages had been opened. A radio message was sent to the control tower: "Monkeys loose on plane." When the plane landed, the monkeys were looking out the windows.

1. The best title is—
   (A) A Wonderful Vacation
   (B) Flying Animals
   (C) Flight Crews
   (D) Feeding Mynah Birds

2. The story says that one animal that travels in airplanes is—
   (A) a gorilla   (B) a spider
   (C) a snake   (D) an elephant

3. The animals that got loose on the plane were—
   (A) monkeys   (B) cats
   (C) dogs   (D) giraffes

4. The story suggests that animals that fly on airplanes need—
   (A) no food   (B) special care
   (C) warm clothes   (D) special beds

5. The word "elsewhere" in line four means—
   (A) no place   (B) other places
   (C) department stores   (D) libraries

Do you save pennies? Lots of people do. In Washington, D.C., a special group of people are trying to *persuade* the government to get rid of the penny. These people want to convince the government that pennies are more trouble to carry than they are worth. Others at the U.S. Mint, the place where pennies are made, disagree. They say pennies are here to stay because most people want them.

Some people think finding a penny will bring good luck. However, they are often thrown out with the trash. In one garbage recycling plant in Florida, workers find $1,000.00 in pennies every week.

Every year our government makes twelve billion pennies. Every year six billion disappear into millions of piggy banks.

---

1. The best title is—
   (A) Pennies—Popular or Not?
   (B) A Good-luck Penny
   (C) Pennies from Heaven
   (D) The U.S. Mint

2. A special group in Washington wants to—
   (A) collect pennies
   (B) get rid of the penny
   (C) toss pennies in a wishing well
   (D) give away pennies

3. Every year pennies are—
   (A) used in board games
   (B) thrown out
   (C) given a new design
   (D) worth more

4. The story suggests that compared to years ago a penny today—
   (A) is heavier in weight
   (B) is brighter
   (C) does not buy much
   (D) is prettier

5. The word "persuade" in line two means—
   (A) help
   (B) upset
   (C) win over
   (D) agree with

On October 24, 1901, Annie Edson Taylor climbed into a big barrel, determined to go over Niagara Falls—and live.

In a few minutes, the 43-year-old teacher from Bay City, Michigan, was strapped into the *cask* and set adrift. As thousands watched, the barrel was swept along swiftly to the edge. Over it went, hurtling toward the pool 160 feet below.

In ten seconds the barrel appeared in the spray and mist below. Shouts and cheers rose from the crowd on the nearby bank. About fifteen minutes later, when the cask was reached and opened, her aide exclaimed, "She's alive!"

The "Queen of the Mist" became the first to go over Niagara Falls in a barrel and live to tell about it.

---

1. The best title is—
   (A) Shouts and Cheers
   (B) The Little Barrel
   (C) Over the Falls in a Barrel
   (D) A Dangerous Fall

2. The story says that Annie Edson Taylor was—
   (A) an acrobat   (B) a teacher
   (C) a reporter   (D) an artist

3. The drop was—
   (A) 100 feet   (B) 160 feet
   (C) 43 feet   (D) 15 feet

4. You can tell from the story that Annie's aide was surprised—
   (A) that she went over the falls   (B) that she lived
   (C) at her determination   (D) that there were cheers

5. The word "cask" in line four means—
   (A) airplane   (B) bed
   (C) car   (D) barrel

What has one foot, likes to move at night, and carries its house wherever it goes? The answer is the snail. Its house is its shell, which grows larger as the snail grows.

The snail's foot is *approximately* as wide as its shell, and it helps the snail travel safely. A sticky liquid is dropped from an opening near the snail's head. This stops the snail from slipping or sliding.

Most snails can be seen only at night, but they sometimes come out after a rainstorm. See if you can find a snail at night or the next time it rains.

---

1. The best title is—
   (A) How to Build a House
   (B) The Snail
   (C) A Safe Trip
   (D) The Snail's Foot

2. The snail's house is its—
   (A) foot　　　　　　　(B) shell
   (C) liquid　　　　　　(D) head

3. A snail's foot helps it—
   (A) eat　　　　　　　(B) travel
   (C) carry things　　　(D) swim

4. You would probably have the best chance of finding snails—
   (A) at night　　　　　(B) after a rainstorm
   (C) at noon　　　　　(D) before a rainstorm

5. The word "approximately" in line four means—
   (A) very　　　　　　(B) more
   (C) nearly　　　　　(D) never

A lot of people worry about the African chimpanzee. Its population in the wild is shrinking because it is hunted to be sold. For every chimp that is taken alive, five to ten chimps die. In the past fifty years, Africans have sold three to four thousand chimps for use in business and experiments. If this practice continues, the chimp may become extinct.

The United States may soon join the other ninety-nine nations that prevent chimps from being bought and sold. In Washington, D.C., the Interior Department *recommends* putting the chimpanzee on the endangered animals list, which will make it against the law to sell them to the United States. Once on the list, they will have a better chance to survive.

1. The best title is—
    (A) The Life of a Chimp
    (B) African Jungles
    (C) Save the Chimpanzee
    (D) The Shrinking Population

2. The story says that chimps are used for—
    (A) movies   (B) TV programs
    (C) experiments   (D) pets

3. For every chimp that is taken alive, five to ten others—
    (A) are born   (B) die
    (C) are captured, too   (D) are hurt

4. For the survival of the chimp, the story suggests—
    (A) there is hope   (B) there is no hope
    (C) nobody cares   (D) no one needs to worry

5. The word "recommends" in line nine means—
    (A) forgets about   (B) hides
    (C) prevents   (D) suggests

Birds are animals that have feathers and wings. We see them flying overhead and resting in trees. However, not all birds can fly. The largest bird in the world, the ostrich, is one of these nonflying birds. It has strong legs that help it run very fast to *escape* from its enemies. Its legs are so powerful that it can kill a person with one kick. Zoo keepers are careful when feeding ostriches.

The eating habits of ostriches are strange. They will swallow almost anything. Keys, nails, wood, and even money have been found in their stomachs!

Ostriches are often raised on farms for their beautiful feathers called plumes. The plumes are used for decorating hats and dresses.

1. The best title is—
   (A) Powerful Legs
   (B) Beautiful Feathers
   (C) The World's Largest Bird
   (D) What Ostriches Eat

2. The ostrich can—
   (A) fly high
   (C) dig deep
   (B) sing well
   (D) run fast

3. Birds have feathers and—
   (A) wings
   (C) hair
   (B) fins
   (D) horns

4. When feeding ostriches, zoo keepers are afraid of being—
   (A) kicked
   (C) licked
   (B) eaten
   (D) fired

5. The word "escape" in line four means—
   (A) take
   (C) capture
   (B) get away from
   (D) catch

When you come across a new word in your reading, you can sometimes get its meaning from the context. For example, in Unit 7 you read:

> Everyone said Levi's *trousers* were the best around, and they started calling them Levis. Today, more than a hundred years later, we still use the same name. We also know the pants as dungarees or blue jeans.

The word *trousers* may be unfamiliar. There are words around *trousers* that give you clues: *pants* is another word that means the same as *trousers*; *dungarees* and *blue jeans* are types of trousers.

A. Exercising Your Skill

Read the sentences below, which are from stories you read in this book. Use the context to figure out the meaning of each underlined word. Write the word and its meaning on your paper.

1.   He [the moose] became friendly with the cows and began staying around them all day as they <u>grazed</u> in the pasture. The moose even began eating with the cows, helping to finish up the grass in the pasture.

    Grazed means: (a) ate grass   (b) walked around   (c) played

2.   Polar bears give Eskimos meat to eat, skins for clothing, and oil for heating and lighting. A boy who can <u>provide</u> all these things has certainly become a man.

    Provide means: (a) talk about   (b) give   (c) find

3.   The <u>custom</u> soon became popular. . . . [Now,] every Easter Sunday a crowd visits the White House for an egg-rolling contest.

    Custom means: (a) costume   (b) practice   (c) story

B. Expanding Your Skill

Compare your answers with your classmates' answers. Discuss the clues in the context that gave you the meanings. Then, using a dictionary or thesaurus, find and write another word that has the same or similar meaning as each of these words: *grazed, provide, custom.*

C. Exploring Language

These words are from stories you read in this book. On your paper, write each word and a word that has a similar meaning. Some of the letters are given. If you need to, you may use a dictionary.

1. damaging   h _ r _ _ u _
2. determined   r _ s _ l· _ _ _ [verb]
3. frequently   _ _ t _ _
4. packaged   w _ _ _ _ e _
5. destroy   _ u _ _

Now use one of the numbered words above to complete each sentence. Look for context clues to help you. Write the sentences on your paper.

1. The company _____ microwave popcorn in special paper.
2. After deciding on a plan, we _____ to follow it.
3. Throwing chemicals or garbage in our waterways will ruin the drinking water and _____ the wildlife.
4. The witness' story at the trial was _____ . His harmful words lost the case for the defense.
5. She often needs extra workers, so she _____ puts want ads in the local paper.

D. Expressing Yourself

Choose one of these activities.

1. See how many words you can "build" by putting together word parts from the list below. Use a dictionary if you want to. List your words on your paper. Then choose five of the words you wrote, and use them in sentences.

in-	use	side	-er
re-	place	take	-ing
mis-	field	spell	-ed

2. Write a short paragraph about a topic that you read about in this book. Use at least four of these words taken from the stories: *disagree, disappear, recommends, produce, practice, continues.* You may look up their meanings in the dictionary.

Do you dream 1,500 dreams a year? That is the number dream *specialists* say most of us dream in a year.

Elizabeth Lowe is not only a dreamer, but a collector of dreams as well. She collected dreams for years. Many people saw her ads in newspapers and sent her descriptions of their dreams. She had thousands of dreams and picked the best ones to describe in a book.

In her book she gives only the age of the dreamer, not the name. She tells whether the dreamer is male or female. Elizabeth does not give meanings to the dreams because the meanings are really up to the dreamer.

---

1. The best title is—
   (A) How to Dream
   (B) Newspaper Ads
   (C) A Collector of Dreams
   (D) The Meaning of Dreams

2. Elizabeth collected dreams from people by using—
   (A) the telephone   (B) newspaper ads
   (C) TV ads   (D) the dictionary

3. Her collection was made up of—
   (A) old coins   (B) rare stamps
   (C) dreams   (D) baseball cards

4. Elizabeth Lowe's collection was—
   (A) ordinary   (B) very small
   (C) on TV every Sunday   (D) not a common one

5. The word "specialists" in line two means—
   (A) champions   (B) experts
   (C) machines   (D) science teachers

Most people think of a desert as flat, completely covered with sand, and without water. All of these ideas are not true. The largest desert in the world is a good example.

This desert, the Sahara, is located in Africa. It is larger than the entire United States. It has several mountains, and great areas are covered with rocks and boulders. Much of the desert, however, is covered with sand. The wind causes the sand to drift into hills called dunes. These sand dunes may be three hundred to four hundred feet high.

It is true that a desert is a dry place, but in certain *regions* there are springs called oases. Desert people live here, and travelers often stop for water and rest.

---

1. The best title is—
   (A) Desert Visitors
   (B) Sand Dunes
   (C) What a Desert Is Like
   (D) A Desert Oasis

2. Sand dunes are caused by—
   (A) sunshine   (B) wind
   (C) rain   (D) builders

3. The Sahara Desert is—
   (A) in Africa   (B) in the United States
   (C) on a mountain   (D) an oasis

4. The story suggests that Africa is—
   (A) flat   (B) cold
   (C) much dryer than the   (D) much larger than the
       United States   United States

5. The word "regions" in line ten means—
   (A) stains   (B) mountains
   (C) places   (D) valleys

Valentine's Day is a favorite day for sending cards to people we like, but do you know how this custom may have begun?

Many years ago, an emperor of Rome wanted more men to serve in his army. He knew that married men did not want to leave home. So he made a *rule* that no man could get married until he had served in the army. Many young people in love were very sad. A priest named Valentine felt sorry for the young lovers and began to marry them. The emperor found out and put Valentine in prison. He died on February 14, after many years in jail.

People in love began sending messages to each other on this date, and today we send many kinds of friendly cards on Valentine's Day.

---

1. The best title is—
   (A) An Emperor of Rome
   (B) How Valentine's Day Began
   (C) Sending Cards
   (D) A Popular Holiday

2. Valentine lived—
   (A) a few years ago   (B) in England
   (C) a short life   (D) long ago

3. Valentine was a—
   (A) lover   (B) priest
   (C) king   (D) soldier

4. When Valentine married people, the emperor—
   (A) was happy   (B) never found out
   (C) became angry   (D) joined the army

5. The word "rule" in line five means—
   (A) habit   (B) discovery
   (C) law   (D) thought

Since the beginning of civilization, people have been sending mail. At first, delivery was only as fast as the messenger or the horse could run. Trains and trucks helped speed things up, but until airplanes, a coast-to-coast delivery could take weeks. Today, you can send E-mail anywhere in the world in the wink of an eye.

The "E" in "E-mail" actually stands for "electronic." But it could also stand for easy, efficient, entertaining, *economical*, and extremely quick! Using your computer, you can deliver a greeting, tell a joke, suggest an idea, or give out important information. You can express an opinion, catch up with a friend, stay in touch with family, or make plans. You can place an order, ask a question, or set up an appointment.

With E-mail, instant delivery is just a mouse click away. Send!

---

1. The best title is—
   (A) Don't Forget to Write
   (B) Getting in Touch with E-mail
   (C) Writing with Your Computer
   (D) How Mail Gets Delivered

2. People have always—
   (A) used computers
   (B) traveled by air
   (C) sent mail
   (D) ridden horses

3. The "E" in the word "E-mail" stands for—
   (A) electronic
   (B) energetic
   (C) elastic
   (D) electrical

4. The story suggests that E-mail is faster than—
   (A) a joke
   (B) your friends
   (C) regular mail
   (D) a mouse click

5. The word "economical" in line seven means—
   (A) practical
   (B) money-saving
   (C) memorable
   (D) fast-moving

Many people train animals to do tricks. Dr. Harold Gorman's way of training animals was out of this world. He trained animals to do tricks in space. At Brooks Air Force Base in San Antonio, Texas, he raised the first animals to travel in space.

Dr. Gorman worked with animals all his life. He invented the first *artificial* hip joint for dogs and then went on to make a hip joint for people.

Years ago during World War II in Holland, Dr. Gorman led a group of animal doctors. Together they saved over a million cattle from drowning when bombs destroyed the dikes and flooded the farmland of that small country in western Europe.

---

1. The best title is—
   (A) Holland
   (B) Space Programs
   (C) Dr. Harold Gorman
   (D) World War II

2. Dr. Gorman trained animals to—
   (A) do tricks on stage
   (B) live in zoos
   (C) go into space
   (D) be good pets

3. Dr. Gorman made a—
   (A) strong dike
   (B) special cage
   (C) hip joint for dogs
   (D) spaceship

4. The story suggests that Dr. Gorman—
   (A) was an astronaut
   (B) loved animals
   (C) was afraid of animals
   (D) traveled a lot

5. The word "artificial" in line six means—
   (A) real
   (B) not natural
   (C) not expensive
   (D) small

Long ago in ancient Greece, a writer named Strabo told about a mystery cave that stood next to the Temple of Apollo. People went into the cave and were never seen again. Only the temple priests were able to enter and return. When they came out, their faces had turned red.

Professor Sheldon Aaronson of Queens College, New York, believes that he has solved the mystery. Near the cave, hot springs produce gases that are *poisonous*. He thinks these dangerous gases may have gotten into the cave.

What about the priests? How did they escape? The professor thinks they held their breath while in the cave. That is why their faces became red.

Today there are bars across the entrance to the cave to prevent anyone from entering.

1. The best title is—
   (A) A Mystery Cave
   (B) Red Faces
   (C) Ancient Greece
   (D) Strabo

2. People who were not priests entered the cave and—
   (A) saw cave drawings
   (B) never returned
   (C) found gold
   (D) got sick

3. Today the cave—
   (A) is a restaurant
   (B) is a tourist hotel
   (C) has bars across it
   (D) has healthy air

4. The story suggests that today the cave is—
   (A) beautiful
   (B) still dangerous
   (C) dark and damp
   (D) very safe

5. The word "poisonous" in line eight means—
   (A) watery
   (B) deadly
   (C) white
   (D) healthy

UNIT 31

Have you ever looked up with surprise at the sight of a balloonlike airship floating and gliding in the sky? Did you wonder what it was and where it came from? If so, you have spotted a blimp.

A blimp is an airship that carries a bag filled with helium gas. Like a giant party balloon, it floats upward because the gas inside it is lighter than the air around it. It *cruises* above the earth at a height of one thousand to three thousand feet.

Blimps are used in many different ways. Some blimps show ads on banners or in blinking lights. Others carry sightseers. Still others are used as camera platforms for TV camera crews. They give all their riders a bird's-eye view of the earth.

---

1. The best title is—
   (A) Riding in a Blimp
   (B) A View from a Blimp
   (C) Blimps
   (D) Party Decorations

2. Blimps can float in the sky because they contain—
   (A) water   (B) helium
   (C) oxygen   (D) feathers

3. Blimps are similar to—
   (A) helium-filled balloons   (B) ships
   (C) rockets   (D) jet planes

4. A ride in a blimp must be—
   (A) choppy   (B) very dull
   (C) too noisy   (D) smooth and peaceful

5. The word "cruises" in line six means—
   (A) travels   (B) shines
   (C) blinks   (D) falls

Have you ever wondered about how certain animals got their names? People often gave animals names that tell how the animal looks or acts.

A vine snake stretches half of its body to make a bridge between branches. When it stops moving, it looks like a vine.

A male fiddler crab looks as though it carries an *instrument* shaped like a violin. What it really is, though, is the crab's one giant claw, called a fiddle.

Spinner dolphins off the coast of Hawaii burst from the water, flip, and spin around before they dive back into the sea.

---

1. The best title is—
    (A) Dolphins in Hawaii
    (B) Names That Describe Animals
    (C) Life of a Crab
    (D) Vine Snakes and Other Reptiles

2. A fiddler crab that has one very large claw is—
    (A) sick   (B) a female
    (C) a male   (D) unusual

3. A spinner dolphin spins around before it—
    (A) goes to sleep   (B) eats its food
    (C) dives back into the sea (D) bursts from the water

4. The story suggests that the people who named these animals—
    (A) never saw them   (B) loved animals
    (C) watched them carefully (D) were not very smart

5. The word "instrument" in line six means something that—
    (A) feeds dolphins   (B) makes musical sounds
    (C) saves time   (D) watches crabs

Jeanie is not old enough to get a driver's license, yet she is a champion car racer. She has won more than twenty races. The cars Jeanie drives are called "quarter midgets" because they are one-fourth the size of *genuine* race cars. Unlike true race cars, quarter midgets cannot be more than eighty inches long or twenty-eight inches high. They are driven on special tracks, and never on streets.

Jeanie built her own car, with her parents' help. The car is built for speed and safety. It contains a small but powerful engine, a shoulder harness seat belt, and a roll cage. The roll cage is made of bars that rise above the driver's head. The roll cage prevents the car from falling on the driver if the car happens to flip over. Jeanie's car has never flipped over, but she likes to play it safe.

1. The best title is—
   (A) A Famous Race
   (B) Jeanie, Quarter-midget Racer
   (C) How to Build a Race Car
   (D) Playing It Safe

2. Quarter midgets are not driven—
   (A) by young people   (B) at night
   (C) fast   (D) on streets

3. The roll cage protects a driver in case a car—
   (A) blows up   (B) breaks down
   (C) flips over   (D) stops

4. You can tell that Jeanie is a—
   (A) silly person   (B) careful person
   (C) shy person   (D) careless person

5. The word "genuine" in line four means—
   (A) small   (B) real
   (C) large   (D) fast

The Arcade Hotel in Ponca City, Oklahoma, has disappeared. It has been destroyed to make room for a newer building, but its history will live forever.

Back around 1910, the hotel was *celebrated* for its good food. A steak dinner cost only sixty cents, and breakfast could be had for twenty-five cents. This does not mean that only people with little money ate there. It was the stopping place for many famous people, such as Presidents Teddy Roosevelt and William Howard Taft, boxing champion Jack Dempsey, and baseball great Ty Cobb. One day in 1911 there were twenty-two millionaires staying there.

So although the Arcade Hotel is gone, it was once a famous landmark whose history will continue to live.

1. The best title is—
   (A) A Famous Hotel
   (B) Famous People
   (C) Cheap Food
   (D) Gone Forever

2. The Arcade Hotel was in—
   (A) Arcade
   (B) Oklahoma
   (C) Utah
   (D) Roosevelt

3. A breakfast at the Arcade cost—
   (A) 60¢
   (B) $1.91
   (C) 25¢
   (D) 22¢

4. The Arcade Hotel was probably—
   (A) very ugly
   (B) unpainted
   (C) not clean
   (D) very nice

5. The word "celebrated" in line four means—
   (A) unknown
   (B) famous
   (C) cleaned
   (D) closed

An eleven-year-old girl appeared on a Canadian eight-cent stamp in May of 1975. She is shown seated, with her head resting on her hands. Who is she and why should she be so *privileged*?

Her name is Anne Shirley, and she is the main character in a very popular book for children, *Anne of Green Gables*. In this book by Lucy Maud Montgomery, Anne is an orphan. All her adventures take place on Prince Edward Island, Canada.

Lucy Montgomery wrote six books about Anne. Would you like to read about Anne? Maybe you would like to visit Prince Edward Island.

---

1. The best title is—
   (A) Collecting Stamps
   (B) Canadian Workers
   (C) The Girl on a Stamp
   (D) Going to the Library

2. In the book *Anne of Green Gables*, Anne is—
   (A) a mother   (B) an orphan
   (C) an old lady   (D) a cook

3. On the eight-cent stamp, Anne is—
   (A) reading   (B) standing
   (C) seated   (D) crying

4. *Anne of Green Gables* has been read by—
   (A) no one   (B) a few people
   (C) many people   (D) adults only

5. The word "privileged" in line three means—
   (A) punished   (B) honored
   (C) happy   (D) sick

Some years ago a person in Alabama was admiring a newly painted house. Then something strange happened. The whole house began slowly sinking into the earth! In a short period of time, the house had sunk into a huge hole.

Such a hole is called a sinkhole. Sinkholes have caused houses, railroad tracks, and even highways to disappear. A sinkhole happens when the roof of an underground cave *collapses*. Some of these sinkholes are dry and some are filled with water. Many sinkholes appear from Pennsylvania to Alabama. In this area there are many underground caves of limestone and gypsum, which are both soft stone. They collapse easily.

1. The best title is—
   (A) Underground Caves
   (B) A Newly Painted House
   (C) Sinkholes
   (D) Houses, Tracks, and Highways

2. One state that has sinkholes is—
   (A) Arizona   (B) New Mexico
   (C) Maine   (D) Alabama

3. One kind of soft stone is—
   (A) limestone   (B) granite
   (C) marble   (D) spongestone

4. Sinkholes happen directly above—
   (A) low valleys   (B) underground rivers
   (C) underground caves (D) drains

5. The word "collapses" in line seven means—
   (A) pushes up   (B) falls in
   (C) grows   (D) dries up

"Please touch!" That is not a sign you will find in many museums, but you will find it in one. That museum is the Ontario Science Centre in Toronto, Canada. The Ontario Science Centre is like a laboratory and amusement park put together. There are more than 450 exhibits, and visitors are asked to *handle* them. In fact, many won't work unless you make them work.

One favorite exhibit of children is the space capsule. They sit inside the capsule and make believe they are in space. The most fun is using the instruments while trying to "fly" properly.

Another popular exhibit is the machine which tells how strong you are.

If you ever go to Toronto, visit the Science Centre and "please touch!"

1. The best title is—
   (A) The Ontario Science Centre
   (B) A Fun Amusement Park
   (C) Flying Through Space
   (D) Don't Touch

2. A favorite exhibit of the children is the—
   (A) weighing machine   (B) space capsule
   (C) science puzzle   (D) old instruments

3. One machine shows how—
   (A) weak you are   (B) much you weigh
   (C) strong you are   (D) much you eat

4. The Ontario Science Centre was built especially for—
   (A) men   (B) women
   (C) children   (D) girls

5. The word "handle" in line five means—
   (A) look at   (B) touch
   (C) destroy   (D) clean

Some animals are not well named. The laughing hyena is an excellent example. Its real name is the spotted hyena, but it is often called the laughing hyena. This is because its cry sounds like a shrill laugh. However, the laughing hyena is nothing to laugh at. It may weigh 175 pounds and be over six feet long. Its jaws are like steel traps. Its teeth can crush the bones of even larger animals.

Many people believe that the laughing hyena is a *coward*. It is true that it usually stays away from larger animals, except when it is hungry. Then it will attack even lions and rhinos. You can be sure these animals do not even smile when facing the laughing hyena.

1. The best title is—
   (A) Never Smile at a Hyena
   (B) What Hyenas Eat
   (C) The Laughing Hyena—A Poor Name
   (D) The Animals of Africa

2. The laughing hyena gets its name from the way it—
   (A) looks
   (B) runs
   (C) sounds
   (D) eats

3. The jaws of the laughing hyena are like—
   (A) a snake's
   (B) a clown's
   (C) steel traps
   (D) a lion's

4. The laughing hyena is most dangerous when it is—
   (A) sleeping
   (B) laughing
   (C) crying
   (D) hungry

5. The word "coward" in line seven means—
   (A) bully
   (B) fearful animal
   (C) helpful animal
   (D) happy animal

The main idea in a paragraph tells what the paragraph is about. Read this paragraph from Unit 31. Decide which sentence is the main idea sentence.

Blimps are used in many different ways. Some blimps show ads on banners or in blinking lights. Others carry sightseers. Still others are used as camera platforms for TV camera crews. They give all their riders a bird's-eye view of the earth.

If you chose the first sentence, you're right. That sentence sums up what the paragraph is about.

A. Exercising Your Skill

Read each paragraph and the sentences below it. On your paper, write the sentence that tells the main idea. Then with your classmates, talk about clues in the paragraph that helped you know the main idea.

1. Some people in business use blimps to carry goods from place to place. Scientists sometimes use them as places to study the air above the earth. Photographers take amazing pictures from the slow-moving blimps.

   • Scientists discover new ways to test the air.
   • Certain groups of people use blimps in their work.
   • Taking pictures from blimps is exciting.

2. A jet flies high above the earth and very fast. A blimp flies low and rarely goes above fifty miles an hour. A jet uses its engine at all times in flight. The blimp's engine is used for takeoff and sometimes for cruising in the sky. It does not burn much fuel. A blimp can stay in the sky a hundred times longer than a jet on the same amount of fuel.

   • Blimps and jet planes are quite similar.
   • A jet plane uses a lot of fuel.
   • A jet is very different from a blimp.

B. Expanding Your Skill

On your paper, write a title for each paragraph in Part A. Then write a sentence that tells why the titles go with the paragraphs. Compare your titles with your classmates' titles. See if any of the titles are alike or similar. Which titles do you think are interesting or catchy. Why?

C. Exploring Language

Read each paragraph. Then, on your paper, write a main idea sentence and a title for each one.

(Title)

1.　　One type of airship is nonrigid and is called the blimp. The blimp does not have a frame. Helium, the gas inside, pushes against the sides and forms its shape. A second type is a rigid airship called a zeppelin. The zeppelin has a frame covered with layers of cloth or metal that is very light in weight.

Main idea: _____

(Title)

2.　　The zeppelin got its name from Count Ferdinand von Zeppelin of Germany. He made a rigid airship that worked better than all the others that came before it. Another name for such a craft is dirigible. *Dirigible* came from a French word that means "able to be steered." Both names are commonly used.

Main idea: _____

D. Expressing Yourself

Choose one of these activities.

1. You have just taken a trip on an airship that set the world's record in size and speed! Write a journal entry describing what you saw and felt. You may write about an imaginary trip, or you may want to read books in the library to find out about a real trip.

2. Draw a picture of a blimp for an advertisement. If you need to, use an illustrated dictionary or an encyclopedia to find out more about what a blimp looks like. Write the ad for this blimp. Give the blimp a name and tell what services it offers, such as carrying advertising banners, sightseers, travelers, or scientists. Use words in your ad that will catch people's attention and interest.

ROBERTS CREEK ELEMENTARY SCHOOL

What spends most of its life standing on its head, eating with its feet, and hiding in a shell? If you look on the bottom of some ocean-going ships, you may see thousands of them. They are barnacles.

A barnacle (say "BAR nuh kuhl") is a tiny animal that attaches its head to a solid object with a kind of glue. It loves to ride on turtles, whales, and penguins, as well as on ships. As it rides along, it sticks out its twelve feet, which grab at small *particles* of food.

Thousands of barnacles on the bottom of a ship can slow its speed. Therefore, these barnacles lose their homes when the bottoms of the ships are cleaned.

---

1. The best title is—
   (A) How Twelve Feet Help
   (B) The Barnacle's Head
   (C) Turtles, Whales, and Penguins
   (D) The Barnacle's Life

2. Barnacles are—
   (A) plants   (B) animals
   (C) ships   (D) shells

3. Barnacles can make a ship—
   (A) go faster   (B) go slower
   (C) look better   (D) sink

4. People who own ships—
   (A) like barnacles   (B) eat barnacles
   (C) dislike barnacles   (D) save barnacles

5. The word "particles" in line seven means—
   (A) squares   (B) bottles
   (C) pieces   (D) cans

Would you believe that some people go to school to learn how to laugh? Maybe you'd like to attend such a school yourself. Have you ever thought of becoming a clown?

There is a clown college run by the Ringling Brothers and Barnum and Bailey Circus. To go to this college, you must first show that you have talent for acting. Every year as many as 6,000 people show interest in becoming clowns.

Those who are *admitted* to the clown college take lessons in acting. They learn how to put on makeup and how to dress up in funny ways. Students must do clever and, sometimes, dangerous tricks. Even if they are sad or afraid, clowns must always pretend to laugh.

1. The best title is—
   (A) Trained Seals
   (B) A School for Laughs
   (C) Going to College
   (D) The Barnum and Bailey Circus

2. To go to the clown college, you must have—
   (A) much money
   (B) poor marks
   (C) many friends
   (D) a talent for acting

3. At the clown college, you get lessons in—
   (A) history
   (B) dancing
   (C) acting
   (D) being afraid

4. To become a good clown, you need—
   (A) ability only
   (B) lessons only
   (C) ability and lessons
   (D) nothing

5. The word "admitted" in line eight means—
   (A) mixed together
   (B) allowed to enter
   (C) asked to leave
   (D) not going

How the turkey got its name is a mystery. It's a puzzle to all who attempt to find the answer.

It is certain that turkeys lived in Mexico centuries ago. Early Spanish explorers took some of them back to Spain, and by 1550, turkeys were being raised throughout Europe.

According to one story, the turkey got its name from the sound it was thought to make, "turk, turk." Another story has it that people confused the turkey with another barnyard bird that was brought from Turkey—thus its name.

Whatever the *origin* of the name, turkey is still the favorite Thanksgiving meal for Americans, as it was for the early Pilgrims.

---

1. The best title is—
   (A) How Turkeys Got to Europe
   (B) The Sound Turkeys Make
   (C) The Mystery of the Turkey's Name
   (D) A Favorite Thanksgiving Dish

2. Turkeys were taken to Spain by—
   (A) explorers
   (B) scientists
   (C) cooks
   (D) teachers

3. The story says that the turkey once lived in—
   (A) Ireland
   (B) Africa
   (C) Mexico
   (D) Germany

4. In America, turkey is most popular—
   (A) on Sundays
   (B) on a holiday
   (C) with children
   (D) with travelers

5. The word "origin" in line ten means—
   (A) outline
   (B) style
   (C) beginnings
   (D) detail

In 1943, Dionisio Pulido, a Mexican farmer, was plowing his cornfield. Suddenly, the earth opened up. Fire, smoke, and lava began pouring out. Dionisio ran to Paricutin, the nearest town, to tell the news. Then he ran to the town of Parangaricutiro. All the people ran for safety. In the next few months, the lava covered ten square miles, and the new volcano stood 1,400 feet high. Both towns had been destroyed, covered with lava.

Today if you visit the area, you will see a strange sight. Where the town of Parangaricutiro once stood is a *barren* field. The only sign of the town is a church tower which sticks up in the middle of the field.

1. The best title is—
    (A) Plowing Cornfields
    (B) Fire and Smoke
    (C) How Two Towns Disappeared
    (D) Running for Safety

2. When Dionisio warned the two towns, he—
    (A) walked   (B) rode a bike
    (C) ran   (D) drove a car

3. The new volcano—
    (A) destroyed both towns   (B) did little damage
    (C) destroyed one town   (D) helped the crops

4. From the story, you can tell that volcanoes—
    (A) are exciting   (B) help farmers
    (C) do much damage   (D) do little damage

5. The word "barren" in line nine means—
    (A) lovely   (B) empty
    (C) planted   (D) useful

What's for dinner? Most times that is an easy question to answer. It's not so easy if you are an astronaut eating food in space. Without *gravity*, food does strange things. It just floats away. Liquids take the form of little balls or one very large ball.

Astronauts used to squeeze their food out of a tube. Later they ate dehydrated foods, foods formed into small cubes by freeze-drying. Now their menu also has frozen and canned food.

Years ago astronauts had nothing to say about what they ate. Today they are asked to choose their own foods. It takes a long time to prepare food for a space journey. How would you like to be asked, "What would you like for dinner eighteen months from today?"

1. The best title is—
   (A) Planning Menus
   (B) How to Eat Dehydrated Foods
   (C) Meals for a Space Journey
   (D) Foods that Float

2. The first astronauts ate food—
   (A) from good restaurants
   (B) ten times a day
   (C) squeezed from a tube
   (D) that came from home

3. Today astronauts are asked to—
   (A) cook their own food
   (B) go on a strict diet
   (C) choose their foods
   (D) freeze foods

4. The story suggests that space meals have—
   (A) gotten plainer
   (B) changed
   (C) no desserts
   (D) gotten worse

5. The word "gravity" in line three means—
   (A) help from others
   (B) spices
   (C) natural force that causes objects to have weight
   (D) natural forces that cause objects to float

There is an animal that has a very strange way of getting away from its enemies—it comes apart!

The glass "snake" is not really a snake at all. It is a legless lizard, but it looks just like a snake to most people. It is called the glass snake because it is as slippery as glass.

When an enemy grabs its tail, the tail breaks off and the glass snake moves to safety. Sometimes it even *separates* into three parts. The strangest thing about the glass snake is that it can grow another tail and be as good as new.

---

1. The best title is—
   (A) Growing A New Tail
   (B) As Slippery as Glass
   (C) The "Snake" That Comes Apart
   (D) Catching the Glass Snake

2. The glass snake is really—
   (A) the farmer's enemy   (B) a lizard
   (C) the farmer's friend   (D) a small snake

3. The strangest thing about a glass snake is that it—
   (A) grows another tail   (B) gets away from enemies
   (C) eats its enemies   (D) looks like a snake

4. The glass snake looks like a snake because it has—
   (A) a small face   (B) small eyes
   (C) no legs   (D) no arms

5. The word "separates" in line seven means—
   (A) divides   (B) joins
   (C) races   (D) hides

Every country has its own customs. Customs are the ways things are usually done. For example, it is the custom in America to shake hands when we meet someone. In some countries, people bow. We have customs with food too. Girls visiting the United States found some of our food customs *curious*.

A girl from the Philippine Islands thought our food was too cold—cold milk, cold juice, cold fruit. A girl from Uruguay thought it strange that we eat so early at night. In Uruguay they usually eat about ten o'clock. A girl from Sweden was surprised that you could buy so many different kinds of food in restaurants.

Customs help make countries different. They make traveling to new countries fun.

---

1. The best title is—
   (A) Eating Late in Uruguay
   (B) Eating in Restaurants
   (C) Different Customs in Different Countries
   (D) Traveling Is Fun

2. In Uruguay, they usually eat dinner—
   (A) at five o'clock   (B) in restaurants
   (C) at ten o'clock   (D) earlier than in America

3. Customs are what help make countries—
   (A) the same   (B) small
   (C) sad   (D) different

4. The story suggests that most food in the Philippines is served—
   (A) cold   (B) warm
   (C) in bowls   (D) uncooked

5. The word "curious" in line five means—
   (A) ordinary   (B) cheap
   (C) strange   (D) old

Did you know that an adult gorilla is strong enough to bend steel bars two inches thick? The gorilla is the largest of the great apes. The male may grow five to six feet tall and weigh from 300 to 600 pounds! The female is somewhat smaller.

Gorillas have some strange habits. They *examine* their food as carefully as a shopper does in a supermarket. They eat mostly plants. Gorillas usually walk on all fours with their hands doubled under. At night the males sleep under a tree, while the females and young gorillas sleep in nests above.

Gorillas were in danger of dying out in Africa. They are now being protected in some areas.

---

1. The best title is—
   (A) The Largest of the Apes
   (B) Protecting Gorillas
   (C) Where Gorillas Sleep
   (D) Bending Steel Bars

2. Young gorillas sleep—
   (A) under trees
   (B) in caves
   (C) by rivers
   (D) in trees

3. The story says that gorillas eat mostly—
   (A) small animals
   (B) rabbits
   (C) plants
   (D) bananas

4. A male gorilla weighs—
   (A) less than a woman
   (B) the same as a boy
   (C) more than a man
   (D) the same as a man

5. The word "examine" in line five means—
   (A) look over
   (B) eat
   (C) put down
   (D) cook

The world-famous Olympic Games include sports that everyone knows, like basketball and skiing. However, at the Eskimo Olympics, which are held in Fairbanks, Alaska, every summer, things are different. The sports are based on Eskimo life—work, skills, and games.

One contest is the knuckle hop. You get down on your hands and knees, as if you're going to do a push-up. Then you make a fist and hop on your feet and your knuckles as far as you can. It hurts.

Another *competition* is the ear-weight-carrying contest. You hang a heavy weight—seventeen pounds—from your ear and walk as far as you can go. The person with the strongest ears wins.

---

1. The best title is—
   (A) The Eskimo Olympics
   (B) Doing Push-ups
   (C) Life in Alaska
   (D) Basketball and Skiing

2. A person needs strong ears to win the—
   (A) knuckle hop   (B) ear-weight-carrying contest
   (C) big ears contest   (D) skiing race

3. The Eskimo Olympics are held in—
   (A) the spring   (B) the summer
   (C) Asia   (D) Alabama

4. The winner of the knuckle hop probably has—
   (A) small hands   (B) no knuckles
   (C) sore knuckles   (D) good eyes

5. The word "competition" in line nine means—
   (A) contest   (B) loser
   (C) corner   (D) city

Circuses are a lot of fun. But one thing that's missing today is the circus parade. In the early days of circuses in America, the circus came to town in a big, big way. The entire circus—from elephants to clowns—would arrive in a long train of beautiful wagons. These were *decorated* with painted or carved faces and animals. Some wagons looked as if they came out of a fairy tale!

Circuses don't use these beautiful wagons anymore, but visitors to the Circus World Museum, in Baraboo, Wisconsin, can see more than one hundred of these colorful old wagons. It's fun to imagine them rolling into town and hearing the children shout, "The circus is here!"

1. The best title is—
   (A) Carved Faces and Animals
   (B) Visiting Wisconsin
   (C) A Parade of Circus Wagons
   (D) Telling Fairy Tales

2. In the Circus World Museum, there are more than—
   (A) five hundred clowns   (B) fifty hotels
   (C) one hundred wagons   (D) seventy elephants

3. Old circus wagons can be seen in—
   (A) Baraboo   (B) Jackson
   (C) Albany   (D) Tulsa

4. The story suggests that—
   (A) there are no more circuses   (B) children like circuses
   (C) no one visits museums   (D) clowns are not funny

5. The word "decorated" in line five means—
   (A) made pretty   (B) raced
   (C) made ugly   (D) cooled

When you head off into the wilderness, it is one thing to know where you plan to go. It is another to know where you are. It can be easy to get lost, especially if trails are not well marked or the weather turns bad. Maps and compasses alone may not help you. But the Global Positioning System in your pack will.

A Global Positioning System, or GPS, is a small, hand-held computer and tracking *device*. It can be programmed with the route you want to take and landmarks you want to stop at along the way. The antenna on the GPS is linked to satellites that pinpoint your location at all times. The GPS can help set you straight if you veer off course.

Hiking into the wilderness need not mean conquering the unknown. With GPS, someone always knows where you are—you do.

1. The best title is—
    (A) I'm Lost!
    (B) Wilderness Camping
    (C) Global Positioning Systems for Hikers
    (D) Going Places

2. A GPS can pinpoint your exact—
    (A) address   (B) location
    (C) weight   (D) route

3. A GPS uses—
    (A) satellites   (B) programmers
    (C) batteries   (D) tracks

4. The story suggests that a GPS is useful for—
    (A) doctors   (B) backpackers
    (C) pilots   (D) shoppers

5. The word "device" in line seven means—
    (A) machine   (B) pad
    (C) vase   (D) van

Every year since 1951, many animals of all different kinds gather for the big PATSY awards. PATSY stands for Performing Animal Television Star of the Year.

All the dogs, cats, camels, bears, horses, and other animals who appear on television programs may enter the contest.

Sometimes the animals get a little excited and trouble breaks out. During one contest, a bull began kicking, which upset one of the horses. The horse fell off its stand and that made the camel, several dogs, a bird, and three tigers raise quite a *commotion*. The stagehand had to drop the curtain, and the show was held up until all the animals calmed down.

---

1. The best title is—
   (A) Circus Animals
   (B) An Important Gathering
   (C) The Exciting PATSY Awards
   (D) Animals for Sale

2. A horse was upset by a—
   (A) kicking bull   (B) runaway lion
   (C) large owl   (D) mean trainer

3. The story says that the stagehand—
   (A) won a PATSY award   (B) fainted
   (C) ran away   (D) dropped the curtain

4. The story suggests that—
   (A) there will be no more   (B) few animals enter
       awards   the contest
   (C) the show continued later (D) the awards are for people

5. The word "commotion" in line nine means—
   (A) contest   (B) program
   (C) fuss   (D) curtain

To answer some questions that follow the stories in this book, you had to make inferences, or "read between the lines."

For example:

STATEMENT: Today there are bars across the entrance to the cave to prevent anyone from entering.

INFERENCE: The cave is dangerous.

A. Exercising Your Skill

Read each of the following pairs of sentences. Decide which sentence is a direct statement and which one is an inference based on the direct statement. On your paper, write the number and the inference sentence.

1. I smell smoke in the house.
   There is a fire in the house.
2. This bread has been left open on the counter too long.
   This bread feels as hard as a rock.
3. I probably got a "B" on that science test.
   I answered eight out of ten questions on my science test.

B. Expanding Your Skill

The five words below have meanings similar to the word *infer*. Use a dictionary to check the meanings. Discuss the meanings in class.

INFER

guess	conclude
suggest	discover
suppose	

Now write the paragraph below on your paper. Fill in the blanks with the five words above.

On some tests you are encouraged to _____ at the answers. People who write the directions _____ that you can _____ correct answers by first identifying the incorrect answers. Or you can use clues that _____ the answers. If what they _____ is correct, test taking should be easy.

Compare your completed paragraph with your classmates' paragraphs.

C. Exploring Language

Read each story below. On your paper, complete the last sentence with facts that you can guess after reading the paragraph.

1. The doorbell rang as I was about to leave. I opened the door. Outside stood two young girls wearing uniforms. A large shopping bag sat on the ground next to them. One girl was holding a box of cookies. She asked me _____ .

2. At the movie theater, people in line were turning away from the ticket booth and going in different directions. They looked unhappy. The show _____ .

3. In the store, Vera walked down the aisle to buy a can of tuna fish. She saw several shoppers grabbing cans of tuna from the shelf and putting them in their shopping carts. By the time Vera got there, all the cans of tuna were gone. Vera said, "Hmm. That brand of tuna _____ ."

4. When Janet lifted a milk carton onto the counter, her hand felt wet. She looked at the floor and saw several whitish-colored spots. The milk _____ .

5. As José walked into the apartment, he wondered why all the lights were out. He was sure that he had left one on. He pressed the light switch, and the room was filled—with balloons, banners, and smiling faces. This was José's _____ .

D. Expressing Yourself

Choose one of these activities.

1. In some advertisements, you see a product and a statement that says exactly what the product will do for you. Many advertisements, however, just *suggest* that wonderful things will happen to you when you use a product. Find three newspaper ads and three magazine ads in which photographs suggest what will happen. For each ad, write a sentence telling what the ads suggest will happen. Explain how you decided on your answers.

2. Create product names for each of these items that suggest something wonderful about the product. For example: shampoo—HairSoClean.

sneakers	snack	radio	jacket	soft drink	bicycle

Compare your product names with your classmates' answers.